THE STORY
OF BREAD

THE STORY
OF BREAD

Prosperity

DEDICATED TO ALL WHO EAT BREAD
IN THIS YEAR OF PROSPERITY ONE
THOUSAND NINE HUNDRED ELEVEN

THE STORY OF BREAD

ERE is a story more than fifty centuries long. But be not afraid. It is squeezed into less than that many pages. For fifty centuries the world stood still—waiting to be fed. Fifty centuries!—think of it—centuries of light, centuries of darkness. Great wealth sat in the high places, great poverty filled the lowlands; the few knew much, the many knew little; the thousands idled and were round and fat, the millions toiled and were cold and hungry; the world moved forward, yet the world stood still.

Man furrowed his brow, bent his back, and crumbled away before his time, all in an effort to scratch from the earth a few grains of wheat with which to keep the spark of life flickering in his starved and shivering body.

"Bread! Bread! Give us bread!" That was the cry. Year after year it was heard. But the world rolled quietly on its way, and the cry was not answered. The wise men were busy gazing at the stars, and those not so wise could not think of a way to more bread.

In the streets of London and Paris, and later, in New York, men, women, and children fought for

thought of it in just this way — few of us have — but plenty of cheap bread oiled the wheels of progress for all time. And as the world had stood still for so many years, its release was a signal for leaps and bounds.

I was about to say that to know the story of bread is to know the story of the world. But suppose we interline this with the thought that to know the story of bread is to know the story of industrial and commercial progress. By its footprints we can follow the path that leads straight from serfdom to independence — from the man in a cave to the man in a skyscraper.

THOSE who have not forgotten their Dickens remember that in passing on the fate of a boat long overdue, Jack Bunsby gave it as his solemn opinion that "the ship has either gone down, or she hasn't gone down." So much for old Jack Bunsby, and so much for the boat. And in like manner, so much for wheat.

Just where wheat came from, and what it was before it was wheat, are largely matters of speculation. It may have come from the valley of the Nile, or the Euphrates, or from Sicily, or from some other place.

As far back as history takes us—which is far enough—there was wheat.

To draw upon the philosophy of Jack Bunsby, wheat may have been this, or it may have been that. Those who know the most about it say that once upon a time it was a wild grass, or perhaps a degraded lily. Recently the thought was projected that wheat is a descendant of "wild emmer," traces of which are found among the rocks of upper Galilee, round about Mount Hermon.

Ages of cultivation, and the experiments of thousands of unheard-of Luther Burbanks have given us the fine large grains which now go to make our daily bread. Enough of these grains were gathered from the wheat fields of the United States in 1910 to make nearly 700,000,000 bushels. Were all these bushels placed in freight cars, and the cars coupled together, there would be two mammoth trains—one reaching from New York to San Francisco, and the other from Regina, which is the capital of Saskatchewan up in Canada, down to New Orleans, in Louisiana, with several hundred cars backed onto the sidings.

Every morning the world wakes up hungry. It has been doing this since the first woman first spoke to the first man. The morning of every day sees the world rub its eyes, stretch itself, push up the curtain, and ask for bread.

We have to learn to eat the oyster, and the olive

REGINA

NEW YORK

SAN FRANCISCO

NEW ORLEANS

and some other things better or worse. But we don't have to learn to eat wheat bread. It is the staff upon which strong nations lean. In point of fact, to eat wheat once is to desire it ever afterward. As the advertisements say, "the more you eat, the more you want." But "there's a reason," to further quote from the advertisements. Nature never does her work by halves, and so she knew what she was about when she dropped that blade of grass wherever it was dropped, or caused the lily to fall from grace and bloom again in the wheatfields of the world. At the same time nature put into man a liking for bread, e'en though history tries to make out that the first couple to set up housekeeping had a particular fondness for the apple. If this were true, would not the exact location of the Garden of Eden be somewhere out West — say in Idaho, or Oregon, or Washington?

We have mistakenly called cotton, king. It is not. Wheat is king, for it contains all the fifteen essential elements of nutrition, and food is more important than clothes. Were one compelled to go through life on a single diet, wheat bread would carry him farther and better than any other one article of food.

Notwithstanding that some people live to eat, all people eat to live. On this point I trust there will be no dispute. But it makes a difference what we eat; for, to recall an old friend, "Tell me what you eat and I'll tell you what you are." Black bread

is — well, it is black bread. True, true, it soothes the stomach and adds strength to the body. But white bread does all this and more. It whets the brain to a keen edge of "get-up-and-get," "twentieth century hustle," and "initiative." Without wheat we would quickly go to seed, just as China has.

In measuring the long strides taken by the American people during the last half or three-quarters of a century, one should not forget to figure in plenty of good wheat bread.

Many a globe trotter has given testimony to the excellence of American bread. You may remember the one who, basking in riches on the other side of the world, offered a hundred dollars in gold for a single loaf. But, alas, there were no loaves. Later he touched home shores, where plenty of bread was to be had for a nickel, but again, alas, and also, alack— he didn't have the nickel.

It was in the United States that wheat raising received its mighty impetus, for it was here the practical reaper was invented and perfected, which made great wheat crops possible, and cheap bread sure.

So why shouldn't we be great wheat eaters? The average amount of wheat eaten by every person in the United States is about five bushels a year. This, passed through the mill, comes out a barrel of flour, and then turned over to the baker is worked up into about two hundred and fifty loaves.

An Englishman traveling in this country at the

time whiskers under the chin — the billy goat variety,
you know — were more fashionable than now, went
home and wrote: "Americans eat so much wheat
that the spears, or blades, or whatever you call them,
grow out under their chins."

Whether the remark was the result of serious
thought, or an effort to be funny is difficult to judge.
One never can tell about an Englishman. But, con-
sciously or otherwise, he paid Americans a lasting
compliment. Prosperity has for its emblem the
spear of wheat, be it displayed in its natural state
or in a decoration for the chin.

But America — large as she is, and great as she
is, and much as she likes to boast — first in invention, first in agriculture, first in prosperity — is not
the only country where great train loads of wheat
are raised.

The sun never sets on the harvest fields of the
world. A writer, with much poetry and some truth
in his soul, penned this: "The click of the reaper
is heard round the world the year round." This
is almost true, and therefore near enough for a
poet—and the rest of us. What he had in mind
was that every day in the year somewhere in the
world, to use the words of the song we used to sing,
they are "bringing in the sheaves." But the click of
the reaper is not always heard. No, not always.
It takes a lot of printer's ink and many strong rays
of light to pierce all the far-off, dark places—little

corners of the earth which for ages have stood still—
waiting to be fed.

To follow the harvest year round the world, be-
gin in January in the Argentine and New Zealand;
in February go to East India, Upper Egypt, and
Chili, and then stay there till the end of March; with
April, drop down into Lower Egypt, Asia Minor, and
cross over to Mexico; May will shift to Algiers, Central Asia, China, Japan, and Texas; and in June the
binder is at work not only in the fields of Turkey,
Spain, and Southern France, but in California, where
big machines are pulled by twenty horses or gaso-
line tractors, and in Tennessee, Virginia, Kentucky,
Kansas, Utah, and Missouri; hot July is the busy
month in the North of France, Roumania, Austria-
Hungary, Southern Russia and England, Germany,
and Switzerland, and, returning to America, in
Oregon, Nebraska, Southern Minnesota, Wisconsin,
Colorado, Washington, the group of Central States,
New York, New England, and Eastern Canada;
August is a little more quiet, but still plenty to do
in Holland, Belgium, Great Britain, Denmark, Poland,
the Dakotas, and Western Canada, aptly termed
"the bread basket of the world;" September brings
harvest days to Scotland, Sweden, Norway, and
Northern Russia and Siberia, where some day
enough wheat will be raised to feed the people of the
earth; October continues the harvest scenes of these
countries; November is divided between South

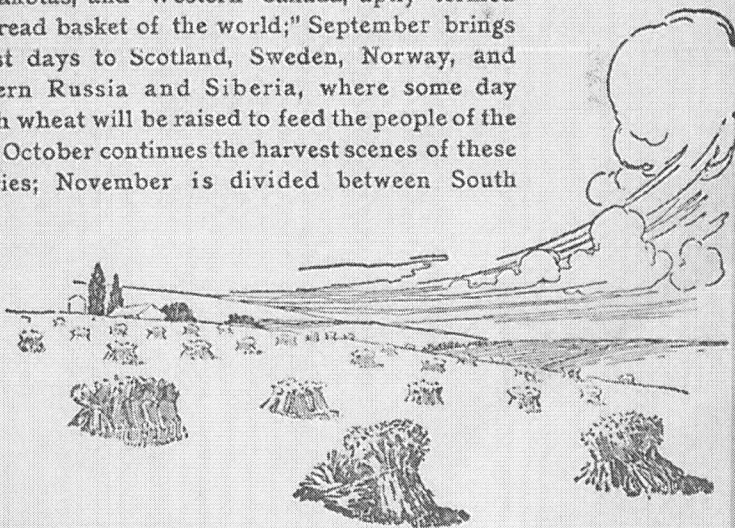

Africa and Peru; December returns the traveler to his starting place — back to Argentine — and thence to Uruguay and Australia for a prosperous holiday well earned.

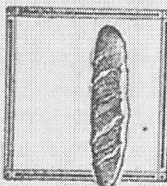

N a lecture which he calls "Acres of Diamonds," Dr. Russell Conwell, of Philadelphia, vividly describes how many people go through life looking for the great thing to do— the momentous deed, the grand achievement, the heroic, the splendid, and all that. They go on looking to the end of their days, all the while stumbling over the most wonderful opportunities—opportunities rich in promise—literally, acres upon acres of diamonds.

A less poetical, if more homely "acres of diamonds" picture may be extracted from our boyhood days, if perchance those days were lived in the country. To come down, or rather to go back, to the point in mind, did you ever go berrying?

You are a boy again. It is morning—just about daybreak. Outside your window another boy whistles. Out of bed you jump, and into your clothes quickly—old clothes, mind you—clothes for the briars to play with. Away you go to the black-berry patch—wild, and tangled, and free—there to

pick the big, fat berries while the dew is fresh upon them. The woods is full of boys—that's the fun of it.

He who skipped blackberry time in the country missed one of the joys of boyhood.

But, as you glance back, do you remember how some boys were all the time running about, here and there, looking for a better place—bushes with more berries and larger? Do you remember? And do you also remember how other boys started in every day at the same place, took the same route morning after morning, and came out at the same point? And you may remember that the boy who went steadily along, picking all the berries in sight, went home with a pail full, while the boy who rushed about looking for the great place, blamed his luck, and wondered why his pail was only half full.

Truly, there are acres of diamonds—even in a berry patch.

Men whom perspective has labeled great, lived and worked, and passed on. They picked many diamonds and strung them for us to gaze and wonder at. And they stumbled over other diamonds, just as large, and just as valuable.

Sometimes we are so close to a thing that we do not see it, and again sometimes we hear a thing so often that we do not hear it at all. These are some of the reasons, perhaps, why the men of the ages did not hear the cry for bread; or, if they heard it, their minds were not in their stomachs, which can't

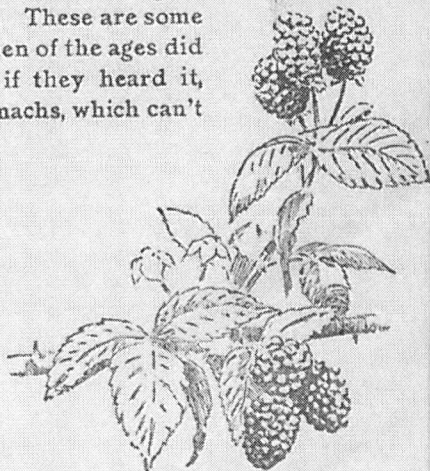

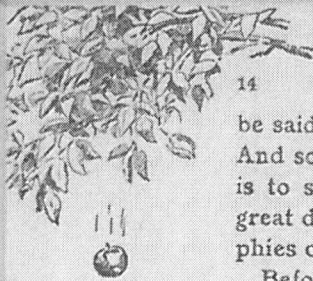

be said of all men, if we are to believe the women.
And so they pulled up their belts another hole (that
is to say, the men did), stumbled over the real
great diamond, and went back to carving philoso-
phies on the tablets of time.

Before a man can work well, he must be well fed;
before he can be well fed, large crops must be
planted; before large crops are planted, there must
be a quick way of harvesting.

This is a philosophy so simple that a child can
understand the truth of it. And yet the brains of
the centuries never thought of this in just this
simple way.

It is rather odd that people should be cramped
with hunger, and yet not rise and say, "Here! we
will find out what's the matter!" In this hour of
system and the working out of the laws of economy,
we are told to do the first thing first. The doctor
relieves the patient, and then cures him. And so,
in working out a plan for the progress of the world,
it was essential that the world's people first be well
fed. But skipping along down the years a goodly
array of talent is seen doing about everything save
the one great thing—finding a way to provide more
bread.

Galileo was busy with the telescope and pendu-
lum, and the poor farmer, Newton, saw the apple fall,
and gave us the law of gravitation. The lid of a tea-
kettle fluttered, as it had been in the habit of doing

since the day fire was first kindled under water, but
Watt was near and turned steam into power. In
América, Fulton used this power to turn the wheels
of a steamboat, and Peter Cooper, another American,
followed Stephenson in England by putting steam
into an engine called a locomotive. Printing was
invented that the world might have more books to
read; but man tilled the soil with a crooked stick
and reaped the harvest with a sickle—just as had
been the way from the days of Boaz—and only the
few had time to read.

Scientists had time for the problem of the origin
of man; but not for the problem of how to feed him.
This was so all the way from Copernicus, the father
of science, to Darwin, who was born the same year
as McCormick. In the Old World, Darwin pointed
back to the trail along which the human race had
climbed; in the New World, McCormick pointed to
the heights up which the race was yet to go.

All the thought of all the philosophers failed to
contribute a mouthful of bread to the hungry; litera-
ture flourished as it never has flourished since;
music marched from master to master, and poets
sang their sweetest songs; art was born and nursed
into everlasting life; soldiers fought and captured,
and again fought and were captured.

Josiah Wedgwood was busy making beautiful
plates in England, whither the art had drifted from
Holland. But he soon discovered just ahead a

greater task than plate making. He had to educate
the public to the use of plates. It was a very difficult proposition to persuade men to buy plates from
which to eat bread, when it was next to impossible
to get the bread. It was very much like asking a
man to spend his last dollar for a pocketbook in
which to carry his money. Wedgwood furnished
plates fit for the Queen. It was in doing this that he
coined the word, "Queensware." But he could not
furnish bread.

Truly, to borrow a line from Dickens, "It was the
best of times, it was the worst of times."

O far as is known, Whitney's cotton gin is the only invention
that ever actually brought on a
war. It so increased the value of
slave labor that the clash between
the North and the South could
not be longer staved off. If it is
true that the cotton gin caused the South to take
up arms, it is equally true that the reaper caused
her to lay them down again. To use the words
of Stanton, Lincoln's war secretary, "The reaper
was to the North what slavery was to the
South." That is to say, the reaper released the
young men of the farm for duty on the firing line

without cutting off the supply of bread, just as the slaves worked the plantations of the South while their masters were away with the army of the Confederacy.

Having played its part in putting a stop to the war, the reaper continues to work for peace. Busy people are prosperous, and prosperous people are happy, and busy, happy, prosperous people do not go about with chips on their shoulders.

The reaper removed the hobble from man's right to the pursuit of happiness. It drove drudgery from the farm, and released two-thirds of the population for the shop, the store, and the office.

And so, to make a long story short, as everybody says but the story teller, the wheels of industry were set in motion, modern business was born, and commerce reached its arms around the world. American civilization pushed westward at the rate of thirty miles a year, and older nations awoke to greatness Railroads came, cities were builded, and inventions multiplied.

Every tall building is a monument to cheap bread.

James J. Hill has said that "Land without population is a wilderness, and population without land is a mob." And he might have added that both land and population without cheap bread are famine and death.

Were it true to-day, as it was a century ago, here in the United States, that ninety-seven out of every

hundred people were kept busy raising enough to eat—were this true today, I repeat, how many skyscrapers, and railroads, and factories, and business houses do you think the remaining three people could operate? Broadway in New York, and State street in Chicago, and Market street in San Francisco would be little more than cow paths, along which a few traders played the game of barter and sell.

We owe everything to something else. Life is one long evolution, in the process of which none escape with their lives. But when we are really ready for a thing, we open our hands and there it is.

Follow a bit. An Italian, Columbus by name, sailing from Spain, found millions of new acres. Freedom, which exists only with the well-fed, hurried an old world people into a world that was new. McCormick, an American, put his reaper onto these acres. About the same time Stephenson, in England, got up steam in the "Rocket;" and Faraday, also an Englishman, harnessed electricity ready for work. There was the line-up. The world was ready. A shout—and progress was off!

The business of railroads is to carry things from where they are to where they are not. And the business of the reaper was to give something worth the carrying. Railroads have been called "empire builders"—they carry settlers and the things they need and use into a new country, and then carry

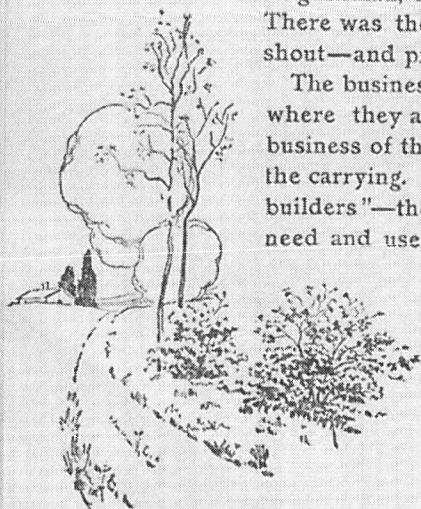

back the crops the settlers and things raise. The reaper had to precede the railroad, just as broad acres had to precede the reaper.

Much is said about the renaissance in arts and letters. Away off in the future some historian, looking for something to write about, will turn to the early years of the nineteenth century as the beginning of a renaissance of happy living—a renaissance of work and play, progress and plenty.

HE Greeks and Romans were long on art, but short on bread. Sit tight, else the jar of the next statement will dump you out. A modern farmer, with the practice of modern scientific knowledge, and the use of modern machines, can with three months' labor raise as much wheat as could an old Roman had he worked ten hours a day, six days a week, for all the weeks of his three score and ten years. In the time of Nero it took four and a half days' labor to raise a bushel of wheat; when the reaper was invented it took three hours; and in the time of Roosevelt it takes ten minutes.

The smallest crop in a new country is not children, and so the reaper came at the right time.

The years have a habit of forgetting those who try—and fail. Somehow, we remember only the successful. So we shall never know just how many tried to think of a reaper, or how few actually worked at building one.

But as the world grew older, the cry for bread grew louder.

Some sort of reaper was used in Gaul, and Palladius, four centuries later, described a similar machine. But they fell into disuse and disappeared.

In the twenty-second year of his vigor—1831, to be exact—McCormick pushed his first reaper out of the blacksmith shop on his father's farm in Virginia. Previous to this eventful year, there had been granted for a similar kind of machine forty-six patents—twenty-three in England and twenty-three in the United States. From this record it is seen that the entire credit for the reaper goes to the English speaking people.

You know there are two kinds of theorists, just as there are two kinds of people, and other odd things. One knows and does, and the other thinks he knows and doesn't do. Parlor discussions are all very well—in the parlor. There is not a particle of doubt but that many of the forty-six reapers worked well in the shop. But a reaper is for use in a field. Hence, the long wait for number forty-seven.

A preacher invented one of the forty-six, a quaker another, and an actor, another. McCormick was a

farmer, and so was his father. Furthermore, his
father had a talent for invention, and so in figuring
out how his reaper worked in the field as well as in
the shop, heredity should not be overlooked.

EW of us ever realize where we are
going. The most we know is that
we are on the way. On the day
that he invested his savings of a
few hundred dollars in oil, had
some prophet whispered to young
Rockefeller that he would live to
give away millions upon millions, this worthy man
would have indulged in the heartiest laugh of his life.
The words "hero," "general," and "Mr. President"
were far from 'Lysses Grant when, in delivering milk
to a neighbor, he overheard the remark that gave
him a chance to try for West Point. Edison, the tele-
graph operator, was making "Edison, the wizard," but
he did not know it. And so without straying further
from the story of bread, McCormick, great as was
his invention, and thoroughly as he believed in it,
did not foresee that he was giving to the world
cheap bread which was to turn the wheels of progress as they never before had been turned.

Every great new idea that has benefited the world
has had to fight for its life. First, we laugh; then,

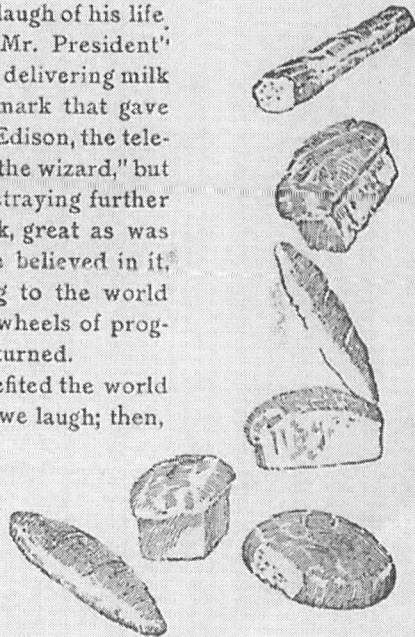

discuss; then, adopt. The leaders of one century
are assassinated that their followers in the next may
erect monuments to their memory. Yesterday, the
authors of new ideas were beheaded; the day before
that, they were burned; and as a proof of how civilization has advanced, today we merely sick onto them
the penny humorists and muck-rakers.

It is so easy to follow along in the old, smoothly-
worn rut.

One would naturally think that with centuries of
poverty, toil, and hunger back of it, the reaper would
have been welcomed with open arms, as it were.
Farmers sat on the fence, watched it work, shook
their heads, and went back to their cradles. And
labor cried that the reaper was trying to rob it of
the right to work. Work! Perhaps you do not
realize just what that meant eighty years ago. In
the hot harvest fields sixteen hours a day at a wage
of three cents an hour. Work! Why, the inventor
of the reaper lived to pay office boys double this
salary for half as many hours.

It is one thing to make an article, but quite another
thing to sell it. The inventor and the salesman are
not always related. Even in this golden age of
industry and commerce, we speak of an inventor as
a genius, a musician as an artist, and a politician as
a statesman. But a business man — oh, he's just a
business man.

Had not McCormick been an inventor, he would

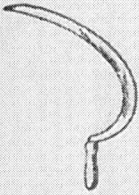

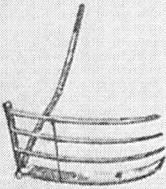

have been a business man, and had he not been both these, he would have been a great general. These three angles, each different from the other, make it rather difficult to get him into this brief story. He had the ability to invent the reaper, then the tenacity to fight for it, and finally, the capacity to market it.

The wonderful foresight (or was it inspiration?) that led McCormick to Chicago is as remarkable as it is rare. Sixty years ago the wheat growing section of the United States was almost entirely confined to those acres nearest the Atlantic coast. McCormick rode from Virginia to Nebraska talking the merits of his reaper. At last he turned his horse to the East, and one day, in 1847, riding into the small city of Chicago, looked about and said: "Here I shall build my plant, for this will be the center of the great agricultural section of the future."

Unlike so many pioneers who have pointed the way and blazed the trail, he lived to see his prophecy come true. And we whom he left behind are seeing more than he ever dreamed his work would lead to.

No longer is the farmer a drudge. Today he is a man who mixes knowledge and science with the seeds he plants and the big crops he harvests. Life on the farm has become so pleasant and profitable that men of the cities are seeking the land.

The words "clod-hopper" and "hay-seed" have

disappeared from our vocabularies. They belong to a time that was. The reaper has made the lowlands rich, has educated the many, and is giving bread and clothes to those that toil. No longer does the world stand still—waiting to be fed.

HE country philosopher who said, "If our foresight was only as good as our hindsight, all of us would do wonders," coined a pat phrase freighted with truth. To look ahead is to see little, to look back is to see much. But when something new is held up, and the laughter is hushed, and the discussions grow commonplace, then everybody sees it. An accomplished fact is so easy to see that we exclaim, "Why didn't I think of that myself?" Then improvements follow. The genius in one man ignites the genius in other men. While more than fifty centuries passed in review before man thought out the right principles of a practical reaper, less than three-fourths of one century slipped off the calendar until that reaper was made a perfect machine.

McCormick's first reaper was crude. But so were his tools. His anvil, for instance, was a large stone. But his reaper, crude as it was, contained the basic principles that are to be found in the modern up-to-

date binder. Time has proved that he was right.
Time proves the worth of all things. Obed Hussey
invented a reaper in 1833. But one great difference marked the careers of Hussey and McCormick
—a difference of something like a thousand miles.
Hussey located at Boston, the center of where
wheat fields were; McCormick located at Chicago,
the center of where wheat fields were to be.
Success sometimes depends as much upon the right
location as upon other things being right. The
location of a bridge changed the hills at Kansas City
into a metropolis, and left Leavenworth, a few miles
to the north, a struggling town.

It took a lot of work to change the reaper into
the modern binder, and also a lot of work to get
the farmers to use it. It was a long, up-hill
fight, and only the hard workers who were hard
fighters live in harvesting machine history. They
were industrial generals, Spartan through and
through.

William Deering was not an inventor. He was a
farseeing business man. But the world owes quite
as much to her business men as to her inventors.

The first binding attachments, like the first reapers, were far from perfect. For the harvest of 1880
Mr. Deering placed on his Marsh harvester three
thousand Appleby twine binders. Taking his
superintendent and chief mechanic, Mr. Deering
followed one of the new machines into a field of

green winter rye. The binder acted very much like the trained goose that belonged to the once famous Dan Rice. It did about everything except the thing it was supposed to do.

Three disappointed machine men sought the little hotel for the night. Afte. supper they trudged up to the one spare room, with two beds.

"Well, boys," said Mr. Deering, "if we cannot do better tomorrow, it means a million to me."

Then bidding care and vexation good-night, he went to bed and slept the sleep of those who fight and win, whilst the superintendent and mechanic put in most of the night talking and worrying over what was likely to happen on the morrow. The next day, after various changes had been made, the machine did the thing it was supposed to do, and once more the sun shone high in the sky.

The first binders bound the bundles with wire. But pieces of wire found their way into the throats of cattle, and farmers tabooed the binder. Mr. Deering's capital and energy are largely responsible for the perfection of a good, serviceable binder twine. This final big step in the evolution of the reaper, made cheap bread doubly sure for all time.

Other men who contributed to the harvesting of greater wheat crops, and who have won the right to live in the story of bread, are D. M. Osborne, Walter A. Wood, C. W. Marsh, of Marsh Harvester fame, and William N. Whitely, once the "Reaper King."

ROAD acres cultivate broad visions. Before one can do big things, one must think big things. Big farms followed the reaper. The cry of "Westward Ho!" was heard. Civilization answered the cry, and farmers watched their acres broaden to "as far as the eye can see."

Men were set thinking. They mixed brains with seeds. Soon they found that hard thinking pays better than hard labor, and agriculture had its rise from "the phases of the moon" to an exact science.

The study of soils, seeds, fertility, insect pests, and the like was taken up, and farming became less a gamble with nature, and more a matter of knowing what to do and how to do it.

Ferdinand Kinderman, a Bohemian, regarded as the father of industrial education, introduced the study of agriculture into his schools in 1771. At about the same time France gave some small attention to the study of agriculture. The first agricultural school in America was the Gardiner Lyceum, established at Gardiner, Maine, 1821. None of these schools, however, did very much for the advancement of agriculture.

The world was waiting for the reaper. With its coming, and the improved farm machines and implements which followed, agricultural education slowly rose to a place of genuine appreciation.

The oldest school of its kind now in operation in America, and the first to be supported by the state, is the Michigan Agricultural College, opened in 1857. But Georgia was the first state to organize instruction in agriculture, the year of this event being 1854. The other states quickly fell into line, and today the science of agriculture is recognized as one of the most important branches of study.

The first experiment station to be supported by the state was opened in Connecticut in the year 1875. Then on March 2, 1887—a date to be kept in mind—President Cleveland signed an Act of Congress which brought into existence the first national system of experiment stations in the world. The United States Government took notice of agriculture when, in 1862, the Land-Grant, or Morrill Act, as it is popularly called, gave to each state a certain amount of land, the proceeds from the sale of which were for the benefit of agricultural colleges. All this opened the way for greater strides in farm work.

Railroads, manufacturing concerns, bankers, business men of every description, all are concerning themselves with the welfare of the farm. A famous banker counting the grains on an ear of corn is a sign of deep interest. But we are not at the end. We are little more than at the beginning. We are just commencing to realize the part good seed, the right preparation of the soil, and other equally important items play in raising fine, large crops.

LUG! Do you know what that means? It means "hang on," "stick to the job," "don't give up the ship," and several other things worth keeping in mind.

To all who think they are having a hard time, that the world is against them, that their efforts are not appreciated, the story of the persistency of the harvesting machine inventors—the qualities which helped to give us bread a-plenty—is dedicated.

From the day the reaper first worked successfully in a Virginia wheat field until a farmer was found who would buy one of the machines, ten years elapsed. It took work and genius to make the reaper; it took patience and perseverance to get it adopted. In the eleventh year a reaper was sold for a hundred dollars. The next year two reapers were sold, then fifty, then a thousand, and on and on, up and up climbed the sales.

Constant plugging away—"Keeping everlastingly at it"—ever earns its reward.

It is an interesting story, don't you think?—I mean the story of bread? In it are symphonies for great orchestras, poems for all who read, and pictures and monuments for all who see.

But best of all, to understand the struggle more than fifty centuries long, is to whet our appreciation of the bread that is so cheap—and, oh, so good.

AND THUS ENDS THE STORY OF BREAD, AS TOLD BY EDWIN L.
BARKER, ILLUMINATED BY GLENN V. JOHNSON, AND PRINTED
AND DISTRIBUTED BY THE I H C SERVICE BUREAU OF THE
INTERNATIONAL HARVESTER COMPANY OF AMERICA, THE
HOME OFFICE OF WHICH IS IN THE CITY OF CHICAGO, U. S. A.

S B.-280 A.

RAND McNALLY & Co., PRINTERS
CHICAGO

IHC
SERVICE BUREAU
SERVICE

LECTURES — "The Dawn of Plenty" (The Story of Bread), illustrated with colored views and motion pictures; "The Builders" (The Story of Business), not illustrated. Descriptive circulars, terms, etc., for the asking.

SLIDES — Sets of slides, with printed lectures, $1.00 per week per set, plus express charges.

OTHER SERVICE — Photographs, 10 cents per print; cuts at engravers' cost; articles for the press, data and information free.

	Single Copies	In Quantities
The Story of Bread	3 Cents	2 Cents
A bright, interesting story of the world-old struggle for cheap bread.		
Creeds of Great Business Men	5 "	3 "
Entertaining sketches of men who helped to build the business world in which we live.		
The Golden Stream	5 "	2 "
A volume of plain, everyday information on the many phases of dairying.		
For Better Crops	6 "	3 "
A collection of valuable articles of everyday use on farm subjects.		
The Story of Twine	3 "	2 "
Tracing twine from the raw fibre to the finished product.		
The Engine Operator's Guide	3 "	2 "
How to operate, repair, and keep in good condition a gasoline or oil engine.		
The Cattle Tick	2 "	1 "
What the tick does to cattle, and how to get rid of it.		
For Better Crops in the South	4 "	3 "
It deals with crops and conditions in the southern states.		
The Disk Harrow	4 "	2 "
Tells how to properly prepare the seed bed.		
The Binder Twine Industry	20 "	15 "
48 pages, done in three colors, showing the process of making twine.		
Harvest Scenes of the World	50 "	35 "
150 pages, handsomely bound, in two colors.		
Plans and Specifications	5 "	per Plan
Blue prints and specifications for farm house, farm barn, power house, machine shed, poultry house, hog house, silo, power house with granary.		

Quantity lots are sent by express or freight collect. Send for a descriptive circular.

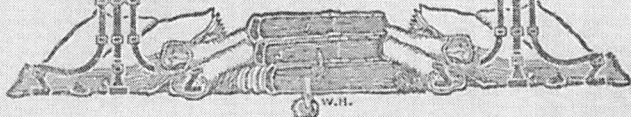

W.H.